101
Shooting Excuses

Bryn Parry

Quiller

First published in the UK in 2005
by Swan Hill Press, an imprint of Quiller Publishing Ltd
Reprinted 2006, 2008

Reprinted 2009 under the Quiller imprint Reprinted
2010, 2012, 2014, 2016, 2017, 2019

British Library Cataloguing-in-Publication Data
A catalogue record for this book
is available from the British Library

ISBN 978 1 904057 74 1

Printed in the Czech Republic

Quiller

An imprint of Quiller Publishing Ltd
Wykey House, Wykey, Shrewsbury, SY4 1JA
Tel: 01939 261616
Email: info@quillerbooks.com
Website: www.quillerpublishing.com

INTRODUCTION

I shoot and there are days when I shoot really perfectly well. I relax, enjoy the company, swing through and knock down those beautifully presented high birds with effortless ease.

There are other days when nothing goes quite to plan. I don't sleep well the night before, get caught behind a tractor, bring the wrong cartridges and the dog does something disgusting on the steps of the host's house. I draw the wrong first peg, miss the first bird and then things start to go pear shaped. The birds sail over my head, I fire both barrels and the empty cartridges pile up.

Remember the 7 Ps. Proper Preparation and Planning Prevents a Pretty Poor Performance. If that fails, have a good excuse ready!

Bryn Parry

I'VE LOCKED MY GUN IN THE CAR

BIT OF AN EARLY START

BIT OF A LATE NIGHT

3

THAT LAST SAUSAGE WAS A MISTAKE

IT MUST HAVE BEEN A DODGY PRAWN

5

TOO MANY CUPS OF COFFEE ...

I BLAME THE SLOE GIN

7

I'VE FORGOTTEN MY GLOVES

I WAS DESPERATE FOR A PEE

TOUCH OF WIND …

I CAN'T HANDLE PORT ANYMORE

I'M NOT SURE ABOUT MY NEW PRESCRIPTION

I'VE GOT A HEADACHE …

13

14   I'M STILL JET LAGGED

I'VE GOT DIS STINKING DOLD

Quite wet underfoot

BLASTED MIDGES!

I CAN'T SEE A THING IN THIS MIST

IT'S FREEZING!

DO YOU THINK MY GUN NEEDS FITTING?

I PEED ON AN ELECTRIC FENCE

MY EAR DEFENDERS AREN'T WORKING

My elastic has gone

IT'S MY NEW GUN

Useless cartridges!

THIS ITCHY SUIT IS DRIVING ME MAD

I'VE SPRUNG A LEAK

MY COAT IS TOO TIGHT

I'M NOT SURE THAT THESE ARE MY BOOTS

I DON'T THINK THE BIRDS LIKE MY TWEEDS

MY GLASSES MISTED UP

I'M WEIGHED DOWN WITH CARTRIDGES

HAVE YOU ANY IDEA WHAT THESE COST?

IT'S A FAMILY HEIRLOOM

MY EXTRACTOR IS STUCK

TOO HOT TO HANDLE

I'M USED TO A LOADER

I SLIPPED ON ALL THOSE EMPTY CARTRIDGES

OUT OF AMMO!

I LOADED A MINI MARS BAR …

I'VE GOT SOME DIRT UP MY BARRELS

I'M HAVING TROUBLE WITH MY SAFETY CATCH

I'M SURE THE BIRDS ARE OUT OF SHOT

MY CIGAR KEEPS GETTING IN THE WAY

IT'S THE NEW HAT

46   I CAN ONLY SEE THE LOW ONES UNDER THIS HAT BRIM

VERY DIFFICULT IN THIS PLOUGH

WELL, THIS IS HOW I WAS TAUGHT

It's easy with a 12 bore ...

49

I'M HAVING TROUBLE WITH MY FOOTWORK

I'VE CRICKED MY NECK PLAYING SQUASH

THE BIRDS ARE A BIT LOW

THE SUN WAS RIGHT IN MY EYES

I'M MISSING INTENTIONALLY ... IT MAKES THEM FLY HIGHER

IT WAS DEFINITELY HIT HARD

DIFFICULT GETTING A DECENT FOOTING ON THIS SLOPE

I'M NO GOOD ON CROSSERS

I THINK I MAY BE LEAVING THEM A LITTLE LATE

I THOUGHT IT WAS 'COCKS ONLY'

I HAD ROTTEN LUCK ON THE DRAW

WELL, IT LOOKED LIKE A PIGEON TO ME

I didn't understand the Briefing

I'M STIFF FROM TOO MUCH SHOOTING

I THINK MY MASTER EYE HAS CHANGED SIDES

THAT BIRD SWERVED! 65

IT LOOKED LIKE MY BIRD FROM THIS ANGLE

I'VE LOST MY KILLER INSTINCT

I THINK MY DOG MAY BE A LITTLE GUN SHY

NO SHOTGUN LICENCE

BLASTED ALARM CLOCK!

MY GUNSLIP ZIP GOT STUCK

I'M WORRIED ABOUT THE KEEPER'S TIP

I DIDN'T WANT TO BE ACCUSED OF POACHING

73

SORRY, I WAS MILES AWAY …

I HAD AN IMPORTANT PHONE CALL

I DIDN'T SEE THAT BEATER

THAT GUN IS DANGEROUS!

MY LOADER TOLD ME TO STUFF MYSELF

ANYONE GOT ANY 16 BORE CARTRIDGES?

BIT OF A BAD HAIR DAY

I DIDN'T WANT TO BE GREEDY

I've just cleaned my gun ... and now I can't do a thing with it

DIFFICULT IN THIS WIND

HER DIAMONDS ARE MAKING THE BIRDS SWERVE

MY DOG DISTRACTED ME

MY WIFE WAS TALKING

I'M NOT USED TO DRIVEN BIRDS

WHAT ON EARTH IS MY WIFE DOING NOW?

MY MASCARA CAKED

I WAS DISTRACTED BY THAT PRETTY PICKER UP

I'M NOT SURE THAT I HAVE TIGHT ENOUGH CHOKES TO DEAL WITH THESE BIRDS   91

MY WIFE RAN IN

I MIGHT AS WELL BE FIRING BLANKS

My wife was flirting with that fellow

I DON'T LIKE TO PLAY THE NUMBERS GAME

I FIND IT HARD TO FOCUS WHEN THERE IS SOMEONE ON MY PEG

IT'S MY FIRST TIME ON BIRDS

MY WIFE SHRUNK MY SOCKS

WELL, I THINK ITS RATHER LATE FOR ANOTHER DRIVE   99

DIDN'T GET MUCH SLEEP LAST NIGHT

I'M JUST A USELESS SHOT ...